AF228191

EXPLORING NATURE

Spotting Mammals

BY LAURA PERDEW

Kids Core
An Imprint of Abdo Publishing
abdobooks.com

abdobooks.com

Published by Abdo Publishing, a division of ABDO, PO Box 398166, Minneapolis, Minnesota 55439. Copyright © 2026 by Abdo Consulting Group, Inc. International copyrights reserved in all countries. No part of this book may be reproduced in any form without written permission from the publisher. Kids Core™ is a trademark and logo of Abdo Publishing.

Printed in the United States of America, North Mankato, Minnesota.
102025
012026

Cover Photo: John Czenke/Shutterstock Images
Interior Photos: William Morris/500px Plus/Getty Images, 4–5; MerlinTuttle.org/Science Source, 7; Shutterstock Images, 8, 16, 17 (person), 17 (deer, bear), 20, 24, 25, 28 (top right), 28 (bottom left), 28 (bottom right), 29; Sarah Laird/500px Prime/Getty Images, 10–11; Dan Kosmayer/Shutterstock Images, 12; Jurgen & Christine Sohns/imageBROKER/Getty Images, 13; Susan Hodgson/Shutterstock Images, 15; Maryia Ihnatovich/Shutterstock Images, 17 (background); Virojt Changyencham/Moment/Getty Images, 18; Mark Newman/The Image Bank/Getty Images, 20–21; Tetsuo Arada/Shutterstock Images, 23 (top); Nick Hawkins/NaturePL/Science Source, 23 (bottom); Gins Wan/E+/Getty Images, 26; Roland Magnusson/Shutterstock Images, 28 (top left)

Editor: Marie Pearson
Series Designer: Marley Richmond

Library of Congress Control Number: 2025939879

Publisher's Cataloging-in-Publication Data

Names: Perdew, Laura, author.
Title: Spotting mammals / by Laura Perdew
Description: Minneapolis, Minnesota: Abdo Publishing, 2026 | Series: Exploring nature | Includes online resources and index.
Identifiers: ISBN 9781098298722 (lib. bdg.) | ISBN 9798384932529 (ebook)
Subjects: LCSH: Mammals--Juvenile literature. | Mammals--Behavior--Juvenile literature. | Zoology--Juvenile literature. | Nature--Juvenile literature. | Ecological science--Juvenile literature. | Habitats (Ecology)--Juvenile literature.
Classification: DDC 590.72--dc23

CONTENTS

Squirrels are very fast. This
helps them escape predators.

Mammals Everywhere!

The chase was on! Two squirrels ran right in front of Raul and Enzo as they walked through the park. The squirrels scampered up a tree. They paused on opposite sides, peeking around the trunk at each other.

One of the squirrels chittered. Then it raced around the tree trunk. The chase continued!

The boys watched the squirrels leap from branch to branch. The squirrels dashed up and down the tree. They ended up tumbling along the ground together in a ball of fur.

Enzo said, "Those squirrels are funny!"

Raul replied, "And they're fun to watch!"

Egg-Laying Mammals

Most mammals give birth to live young. However, there are five **species** that lay eggs. Four of the species are echidnas and one is the platypus. These animals are found only in New Guinea and Australia. Once the eggs hatch, the females feed their young with milk like other mammals.

What Is a Mammal?

Squirrels are one of about 6,800 species of mammals in the world. Humans are mammals too! Mammals range in size. The huge blue whale can be almost the length of 2.5 school buses. The bumblebee bat is just 1 inch (2.5 cm) long. A mammal is a warm-blooded animal with a backbone. All mammals have hair or fur. Most mammals birth live young instead of laying eggs. They nurse their young with milk.

Spending time outdoors in nature helps improve mental health.

Mammals live on every continent in many different **habitats**. Some, such as whales and dolphins, even live in the ocean. Mammals move by swimming, hopping, digging, walking, running, gliding, climbing, and swinging. Bats even fly!

If people look, they can spot mammals almost anywhere. Seeing mammals connects people to nature. People learn about mammals by watching their behavior. There's a lot to love about spotting mammals!

Deserts are among the many habitats where coyotes thrive.

CHAPTER 2

Looking for Mammals

People can spot mammals anywhere. The type of mammal they see depends on the habitat. In the desert, someone might spot a pack of coyotes. In the ocean, a pod of whales may swim by a boat. People might spot a bear in the forest.

And in mountain towns, elk or moose may walk down the street. Mammals can even be spotted in **urban** parks.

To find mammals, people look for signs of their presence. Tracks, trails, fur, **scat**, and gnawed branches are all signs that animals

A bear's tracks show five toes per paw. The prints of the back paws are longer than the prints of the front paws.

have been in an area. People can also look for signs of dens and shelters. There might be a squirrel nest on a branch. Sometimes raccoons use hollows in trees for shelter. Lower to the ground, there might be holes for dens or burrows. The opening to a prairie dog burrow is a mound with a hole in the middle.

Timing

The weather, time of day, and season affect the types of mammals that people see. Many mammals are active at dawn and dusk. At these times, people might see rabbits, deer, and bobcats. Chipmunks are out during the day. People are too! Bats emerge to feed at night. Mammals such as opossums and skunks are active at night too.

Respecting Mammals

People should always keep their distance from wild animals. This keeps both people and animals safe. People should also not disturb or feed animals. When people head into wild places, their pets should stay at home or on a leash.

Eastern cottontail rabbits are often found on lawns, where they can watch for predators. They stay close to tall grasses and other plants they can hide in.

As the seasons change, people can see different animals. Some animals, such as bears and marmots, **hibernate** during the winter.

Places high above sea level are colder than lower ground. Animals may need to move down mountains during winter to stay warm and find food.

Beavers stay in shelters of branches and mud in frozen ponds. Animals such as elk may move down a mountain during the winter to avoid deep snow.

A Safe Distance

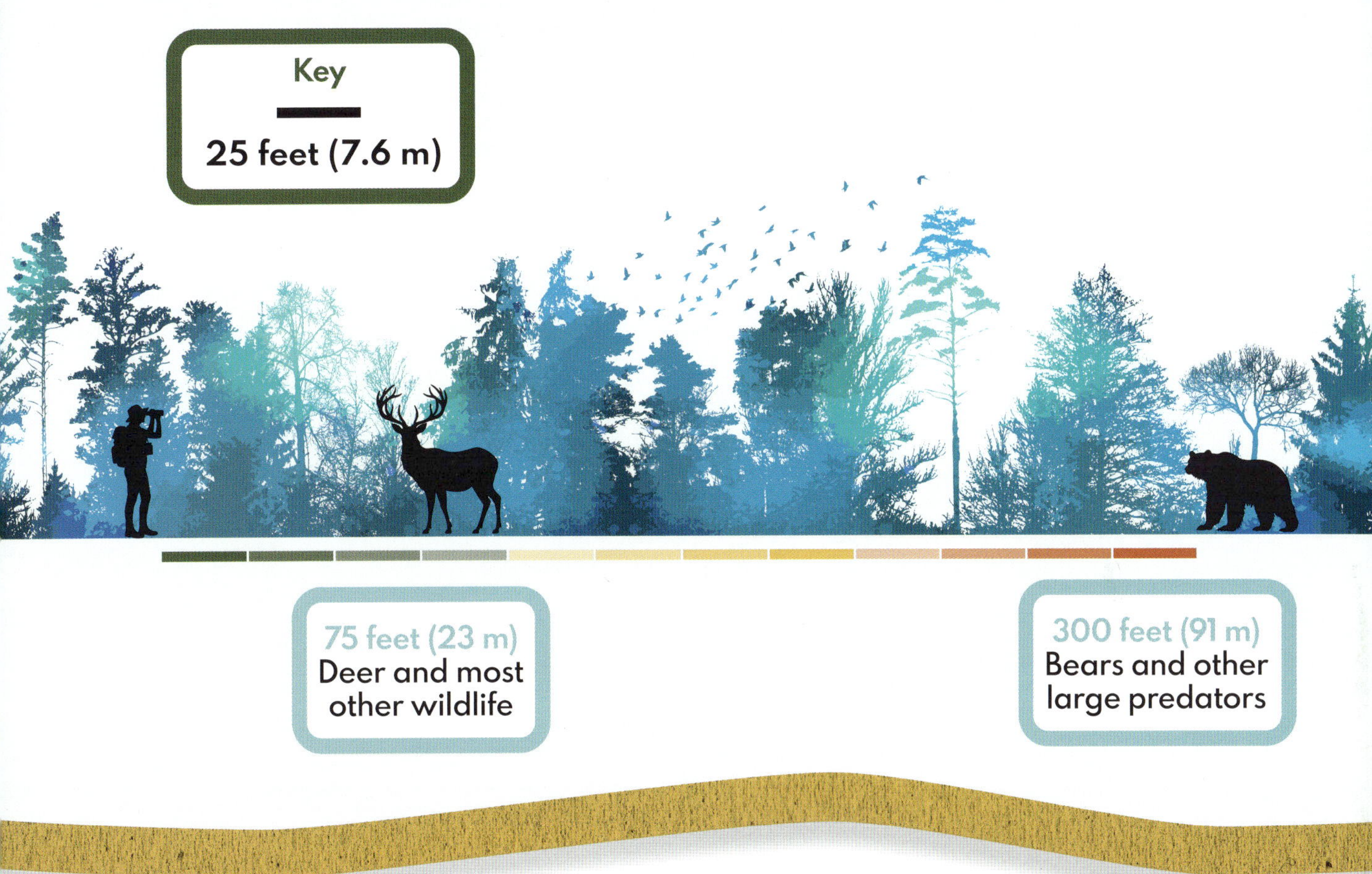

People should stay 75 feet (23 m) away from most wildlife. However, many large animals and predators need more space. For them, staying at least 300 feet (91 m) away is best.

Some mammals **migrate** seasonally. For example, whales make long-distance trips between summer and winter. Animals migrate to find food, to mate, and to find better weather.

Binoculars help people see mammals from a safe distance.

Helpful Hints for Spotting Mammals

One tool for spotting mammals is patience.

Mammals may not be visible right away.

People must look closely. It helps to sit quietly

and not move. Noise and motion can keep mammals away.

People who want to watch wildlife often carry binoculars. Other people carry cameras with a zoom lens to get a closer look and to take pictures. People may also bring along a journal or sketchbook to record what they see. This information helps to identify the mammal later.

Explore Online

Visit the website below. Does it give any new information about how to watch wildlife responsibly that wasn't in Chapter Two?

Principle 6: Respect Wildlife

abdocorelibrary.com/spotting-mammals

The Canada lynx, *left*, is gray and has large feet. The bobcat, *right*, has more distinct spots and smaller feet.

CHAPTER 3

Identifying Mammals

Some mammals are easy to identify. Other times, it is hard to tell mammals apart. For example, lynx and bobcats look similar. One of the best ways to identify the correct animal is by location. Lynx are spotted in mountainous and snowy places.

Bobcats are found in many habitats and are more often seen. The time of day and season also give clues to identifying a mammal.

Ear and tail shapes can help identify a mammal. Fur color and markings help too. Other clues are size and body shape. For instance, people often confuse dolphins and porpoises with each other. A dolphin has a long, pointy snout. A porpoise has a rounded snout.

Marine Mammals

Marine mammals are similar to mammals that live on land. But they spend part or all of their lives in the ocean. Examples of marine mammals are whales, dolphins, seals, sea otters, and manatees.

The bottlenose dolphin, *top*, has a longer snout than the harbor porpoise, *bottom*.

Sea lions sometimes gather in large groups to sun themselves on piers along the West Coast of the United States.

People observe a mammal's behavior to identify it. Some animals, such as seals, most often appear alone. Other mammals, such as sea lions, appear together in pairs or larger groups. When identifying a mammal, people also note what the animal is doing, how it moves, and what it eats. They listen to the sounds the animal makes. Seals are mostly quiet. But a colony of sea lions is very noisy!

Resources for Mammal Watchers

People carry field guides to help identify mammals. Some have photos of all the animals in a region. Field guides can provide information about scat and tracks. Parks sometimes have booklets about animals visitors might see. Online sources may help identify animals by picture or description.

Field guides include pictures of animals. People can compare the pictures with the animals they see to identify them.

Apps and online databases help people find and identify mammals. People can add photos of animals they see. This information helps scientists learn more about mammals and their behavior. It's fun to look for mammals, whether right outside the door or in the wild!

Mammal watcher Jon Hall states:

> When I'm looking at mammals, it's . . . this intense moment of joy. . . . [Mammal watching is] about getting outside, searching for, and appreciating the world's six and a half thousand species of mammals.

Source: United Nations Development Programme—UNDP. "Mammal Watching." *Facebook*, 21 May 2023, facebook.com. Accessed 22 May 2025.

Point of View

What is the author's point of view on mammal watching? What is your point of view? Write a short essay about how they are similar and different.

Field Notes

Binoculars

Camera

Backpack
with water
and snacks

Logbook or journal

Mammal Log

Name of mammal:
Red fox

Date and time spotted:
June 3, evening

Habitat where spotted:
Neighborhood park

Size and body shape:
The size of a small dog; dog-shaped body

Sketch:

Face and ear shape:
Long, pointy nose and large, upright ears

Color and patterns:
Red body with black legs, ear tips, and nose; white tail tip

Tail shape:
Long and bushy

Behavior notes:
Trotting across a clearing

A blank Mammal Log is available at **abdocorelibrary.com**.

Glossary

habitat
the natural environment where a plant or animal lives

hibernate
to spend the winter in a deep resting state

migrate
to move regularly from one place to another

scat
animal poop

species
a group of similar living things that can produce young with one another

urban
describing a city

warm-blooded
able to control one's own body temperature internally

Online Resources

To learn more about spotting mammals, visit our free resource websites below.

Visit **abdocorelibrary.com** or scan this QR code for free Common Core resources for teachers and students, including vetted activities, multimedia, and booklinks, for deeper subject comprehension.

Visit **abdobooklinks.com** or scan this QR code for free additional online weblinks for further learning. These links are routinely monitored and updated to provide the most current information available.

Learn More

Drimmer, Stephanie Warren. *Ultimate Mammalpedia.* National Geographic, 2023.

Hestermann, Bethanie, and Josh Hestermann. *Ocean Animals for Kids.* Rockridge, 2021.

Index

About the Author

Laura Perdew is an author coach, presenter, and former teacher and the author of more than 50 fiction and nonfiction books for kids. Her books highlight the wonders of nature and the environment and call for action to preserve it. She lives in Boulder, Colorado, a great place for spotting mammals!